SO...

The ABC's for Blessed Success

To Diane:
Thank you for blessing
me with 11 years of
friendship and fellowship!
Keep allowing God to use
you mightily.
Tracy

Tracy Mitchell

Scripture quotations marked (ESV) are taken from *The Holy Bible, English Standard Version*® (ESV®). Copyright © 2001 by Crossway, a publishing ministry of Good News Publishers. All rights reserved.

Scripture quotations marked (MSG) are taken from THE MESSAGE, copyright © 1993, 1994, 1995, 1996, 2000, 2001, 2002 by Eugene H. Peterson. Used by permission of NavPress. All rights reserved.

Scripture quotations marked (NIV) are taken from the Holy Bible, *New International Version*®, NIV®. Copyright © 1973, 1978, 1984 by Biblica, Inc.™ Used by permission of Zondervan. All rights reserved worldwide, www.zondervan.com

Printed and bound in the United States of America

ISBN-13: 978-0998745701

ISBN-10: 0998745707

This book is dedicated to:

My mother, Doris "Cookie" Mitchell, who leaves a legacy in pursuing excellence in all that I do and being my greatest example of a woman seeking to please God. Mom, I thank you for teaching me that as a child of God, possess great value and worth, and my life has meaning and purpose. Thus, I must live life to the fullest!

Letter to Women of Color

Dear Beloved:

SonKissed is inspired by my mother, aunts, and grandmothers who planted seeds of wisdom within me as a child. I pray that my message of courage and perseverance will leave a legacy of successful and prosperous women of color who will continue to carry this torch and empower future generations to greatness. I am writing to provide women of color of all ages many crucial lessons that I have learned through life experiences.

You, yes you, possess the power to be all that you desire to be. By the power of the Holy Spirit, you lack nothing and have unlimited potential to soar beyond the clouds. Life will throw many obstacles in your journey to detour you or destroy you. You must be willing to follow the ABC's recommended to reach your final destination of sustainable success (success lasting generation after generation).

Can you stand the pressure? Can you stand the ridicule and rejection? Can you stand the jealousy and envy from your fellow brothers and sisters? Can you stand your own self-hate?

Can you stand the pain of discipline and consistency? Can you continue to get up, and stand again after falling and falling and falling?

Women of Color are a special breed of uniquely gifted and talented beings who continue to rise above in the midst of racism, sexism, classism, and every other bias or prejudice brought against us. Women of Color include a broad spectrum of various ethnic backgrounds including African, Latina, Asian, Native American, Indian, and many others. As a woman of color, I have been judged, criticized, ostracized, demeaned, attacked, and at times made to feel inadequate and unworthy in the 21st century. I have chosen to channel all the negativity in a productive and meaningful way: using my lessons to empower women of color to thrive. Sisterly,

Tracy Mitchell

Foreword

Don't you dare be ashamed of your light or dark hue; your tightly coiled tresses; your nappy afro that's flat on one side; and your full lips and hips. Maybe you're just considered different because you are socially awkward; look, act, or sound white; considered bourgeois; too pushy or cocky for a woman; too short or tall; thick, or thin; too pretty or not pretty enough, or just not good enough.

Brace yourself. It's ALL LIES and a trick of the enemy to make you feel like a failure, lose all hope and faith, and quit or even feel like you have no value, no purpose, and no meaning for your life! Women of Color have been KISSED by the Son of God, our Savior Jesus Christ who gives eternal life, love, joy, peace, favor, healing, and restoration. We have received the "Mighty Kiss" of the Holy Spirit who leads, guides, protects, and provides for our EVERY need.

Take delight in the Lord by feasting on his word, being obedient to his commands, serving Him wholeheartedly, and watch as He Transforms your entire being.

This Heavenly SonKiss is like no other. It is filled with passion and great intimacy; it requires ongoing chemistry and overwhelming emotion. It is very deep, long, yet gentle and warm.

God never takes his eyes off of you and always keeps you safe as He holds you securely in His arms. God's kiss always reminds us that as women of color: we matter, we are daughters of royalty, our lives have great purpose and high value, and each of us has a divine destiny that will be manifested. Nothing and no one will stop us (Many have tried and failed!) However, our victory (in Jesus) will prevail!

As one of God's messengers on Earth, I am going to share my testimony about how God is using my life to shine and give light to other women of color. I always wanted another successful woman of color to help lead me to blessed success. Sadly, it never happened. I learned that most people are looking to help only themselves. They are not concerned with helping you or me. My parents taught me to advocate for myself and others who cannot help themselves.

Moreover, many of them proclaimed to be saved and loved the Lord, but the fruit didn't match the vessel. So, God whispered in my ear and said: "Step up and do it yourself." I have chosen you to be the light for your sisters. I have given you everything you need by my word, your experiences, and people who I have sent to be a blessing to you. He said I'll make it as easy as ABC.

x

Table of Contents

Chapter 1

A-Arise and Take Action

"Arise, for it is your task, and we are with you:
be strong and do it."- Ezra 10:4 (ESV)

Reflection Questions
   (1) What are you willing to commit to doing or
       changing to arise, take action, and lead to
       success?
   (2) How are you going to get it done?
   (3) When are you going to start?

As Women of Color, we must arise and get out of bed immediately. We must get on our knees to pray, meditate with God, and then study His word.

Activate your life by spending quality time with the Savior Christ. This is our #1 daily priority because He is the Reason for our very existence. Allow yourself 15-30 minutes of extra time to prepare for your day and plan to arrive 30-60 minutes early to your destination. If you are joining an important conference call or meeting, it is imperative that you join at least 5-10 minutes prior to the actual start time. Proper planning and preparation are the key components that can make or break you.

In this day and age, being on time is now considered being late or tardy. Tardiness or being a "No Show" is equivalent to bad character and is never acceptable behavior (personal or professional) for women of color. We are called to a higher standard of excellence and will always be accountable to meet and/or exceed our promises and commitments.

The only exceptions are when matters are emergent, require communication in advance, and should be a rare occasion as life is unpredictable. Commit to completing at least one actionable goal or task daily. Write it down and keep it in front of you until done. Then repeat and slowly begin to add more goals or tasks as you can handle at one time remembering to never overwhelm yourself.

You must be able to prove to yourself that you are successful with the little before you can become successful with more. Taking action requires both rest (6-8 hours of sleep per night) and energy (consuming breakfast with protein every day, no skipping allowed). Tune out distractions by listening to soothing or inspirational music, reading, or writing to help stimulate your brain, and/or singing in the shower.

Maximize your morning by creating and following a consistent and personalized routine that works for YOU. Try out different morning routines until you find the one that works best for you and then stick with it. Share your morning successes (as led by the Holy Spirit) to help someone else to arise and take action.

SonKiss Affirmation:
I will arise and take action by…

(Fill in the blank with your personal statement. Repeat aloud several times until you believe it and commit to it. Post the message on your wall or mirror.)

Chapter 2

Bite the Bullet

"In this you rejoice, though now for a little while, if necessary, you have been grieved by various trials, so that the tested genuineness of your faith, more precious than gold that perishes though it is tested by fire, may be found to result in praise and glory and honor at the revelation of Jesus Christ." -1 Peter 1:6-7 (ESV)

Reflection Questions
    (1) In what ways are you choosing to "bite the bullet"?
    (2) How will you apply the lessons you've learned?

To "bite the bullet" means to force yourself to perform an unpleasant or difficult action or to be brave in a difficult situation[1]. From a historical perspective, many doctors would give soldiers a bullet to bite on while they performed operations without pain medications. Women of Color must be willing to suffer, learn from, and most importantly to apply the lessons of life's obstacles, trials, setbacks, and storms that are guaranteed to

---

[1] Merriam Webster online dictionary.

meet us on our journey filled with mountains and valleys.

Choose to endure the pain and sacrifice today and reap the reward tomorrow. When they lie and cheat on you, keep going. When they mock you, keep going. When they use you, keep going. When they betray you, keep going.

Did you notice the word "when" and not "if"? And I'm sure you're wondering who are "they"? Good question. There is never an "if" and there is always a "when." We are meant to be tested just as Jesus was tested. "They" are anyone and anything that comes against you to block or delay your blessings.

It is wise to use great discernment and prayer with everyone you encounter because "they" are not always obvious. Human Beings are generally fickle and can change on you at any given moment. Thus, "They" can include family, friends, church members, co-workers, etc. "They" also include others who do not even know you and may hate on you because they hate themselves. Women of Color will always respond in love and respect to everyone.

In the midst of your storms, remember there is purpose and destiny connected to your coming out of your storms. Every storm has hidden value that applies to improving some area in your life. Women of Color must dig deep to discover that value. Every storm also has an expiration date. God will take you through and bring you out as pure refined gold!

SonKiss Affirmation:
I will Bite the Bullet by...

(Fill in the blank with your personal statement. Repeat aloud several times until you believe it and commit to it. Post the message on your wall or mirror.)

Chapter 3

C-Consider the Costs

"For which of you, desiring to build a tower, does not first sit down and count the cost, whether he has enough to complete it?"
- Luke 14:28 (ESV)

Reflection Questions
(1) What are the costs you must consider to manifest your God-given dreams?
(2) In which ways are you avoiding or procrastinating in your God-given dreams, negatively affecting your future and many others connected to your purpose?

Women of color, what do you want? God has gifted each of us with unique skills and experiences equipped to align us with reaching our destiny. Have you ever taken the time to envision your God-given dreams and consider the costs for what you want?

In case you are not aware, there is a huge cost to following Jesus. We are not allowed to be selfish and do whatever we feel when we want to and how we want to do it. It's much more than just lip service as it is representative of a daily lifestyle where we choose to live righteously and according to the word and will of God.

The greatest evidence is in what we do behind closed doors when no one is watching us. This illustration closely relates to principles in business success. The costs include time, money, priority management, tools and resources, training, education, experiences, setting and reaching measurable and time sensitive goals, business action plan, marketing and networking, budgeting, and a mentor or coach who can help you plan and prepare for successful outcomes.

The costs also include a hunger for greater, a helping hand willing to serve, and a humble heart willing to walk in integrity at all times. How bad do you want it? Are you willing to endure rejection, misunderstanding, gossip, humiliation from failure over and over again, getting no's and slammed doors in your face, sleepless nights, hungry days, potential health risks, loss of time, money, property, relationships, etc.?

We only know of the stories of the ones who made it because through it all, they never gave up. Though the costs may be great, the ROI (Return on Investment) is life transforming as God rewards you exceedingly and abundantly for your faithfulness. If you want it bad enough, it's worth it to consider all the costs and never quit until you are finished.

SonKiss Affirmation:
I will Consider the Costs by…

(Fill in the blank with your personal statement. Repeat aloud several times until you believe it and commit to it. Post the message on your wall or mirror.)

Chapter 4

D-Release the Dead Weight

"Come to me, all who labor and are heavy laden, and I will give you rest. Take my yoke upon you, and learn from me, for I am gentle
  and lowly in heart, and you will find rest in your souls. For my yoke is easy, and my burden is light."
- Matthew 11:28-30 (ESV)

Reflection Question:
  (1) What are some of the areas of dead weight that you must release?

It's time for us to release all of the Dead Weight in our lives: Toxic people who mean you no good, Lack, Less Than, or Not Good Enough Mentality, Limited
Mindset/Thinking, Places holding us in bondage, Things causing stagnation, Time wasters, Prolonged Season with the wrong people such as leeches sucking the life out of you, moochers draining your wallet, users, haters, and dysfunctional enablers unable to realize they are hurting and not helping by not allowing you to take blame or responsibility for your own actions.
  Here's a rule of thumb: If it is not helping you to grow, it's time to let it go. If there is no life in it,

leave it alone. Create a new daily life pattern in which you slowly allow yourself to avoid the people, places, and things that are no longer purposeful and life fulfilling.

This may include avoiding phone calls, outings, saying "no", spending some time alone, and may also include meeting new people and finding new hobbies. Here's an exercise that may help: Think about why you act and think the way that you do. Spend some time reflecting with family, trusted friends, church leaders, or a licensed therapist on your behaviors and patterns, both positive and negative.

Choose to reinforce and further develop the positive behaviors and patterns. Regarding the negative behaviors patterns, serve them an eviction notice by deciding that you want to be all that you can be in Christ and you are willing to face and deal with your demons, struggles, negative emotions, fears, addictions, pain, etc. It will not be easy but it is necessary and mandatory that anything not of Christ... MUST GO!

Jesus desires to set you free and give you new life. There is never a need for you to carry excess baggage when Jesus is always available to heal and restore you. Give every part of you to Christ and let Him rebuild you Brand New.

If you find yourself having difficulty releasing a dead weight and/or re-igniting a dead weight you were previously freed from, do not hesitate to reach out to family, trusted friends, or a leader in your church (using discernment and discretion accordingly), seek professional counseling or therapy, if applicable, and always go into prayer, fasting, and worship to the Lord.

SonKiss Affirmation:
I will Release my Dead Weight by…

(Fill in the blank with your personal statement. Repeat aloud several times until you believe it and commit to it. Post the message on your wall or mirror.)

Chapter 5

E-Expect the Unexpected

"Trust in the Lord with all your heart, and do not lean on your own understanding. In all your ways acknowledge him, and he will make straight your paths."- Proverbs 3: 5-6 (ESV)

Reflection Questions:
(1) What are some of the old mindsets and unrealistic expectations that you must remove to become unstoppable?
(2) What are some of the new mindsets and lifestyle changes that you plan to embrace and tap into to become unstoppable?

One of the biggest life lessons God has taught me is to "Expect the Unexpected." Once I received that miraculous epiphany, I became a new me by challenging my old way of living, thinking, and acting by choosing what would benefit my greater purpose.

Let's just say I begin to have an "Out the Box" living experience. I now questioned and researched everything before my eyes and ear gates because western society had played a part in brainwashing and desensitizing my living experience. There were many images and messages that I had repeatedly received which internally had made me believe that something was wrong with me. In the midst of this ongoing madness, God gave me a mother who instilled in me great values of wisdom and self -worth as a child.

Long after my mother's death, I can clearly hear my mother's words (seeds planted in my head) and they carry me through when I become lost or fearful. Then in my adult life, God began enlightening me to an existence in which He had blessed me with everything I need and I already possessed the power to be Unstoppable! I just did not realize it and now had the choice to tap into it if I so chose.

Now I'm knowledgeable that Life will not make sense at times. We must trust God and continue to obey when it does not make sense and remember that he is orchestrating in our favor behind the scenes. I expected to go to college, get married, start a family, and be active in my community because that's all I was exposed to.

But that didn't happen how or when I expected. Thus, I begin to feel like a failure for not living up to my (limited) unrealistic expectations beyond my control. I never expected that I would become a nurse, business owner, author, speaker, coach, trainer, be able to travel internationally, share and give my heart to empower other beautiful women of color, and leave a legacy that women of color can and will continue to Thrive! I almost suffered a nervous breakdown when I failed in nursing school and lost my scholarship. I now realize that Failure is a required component in advance of succeeding.

This was a normal part of my process that I was not aware of at that time in my life. This life lesson also taught me that I must remain flexible, be open to change, keep failing until you find what works, and stay prepared because opportunities can arrive at any time.

Women of color, I challenge you to remove your unrealistic expectations, your life plan & timing, preconceived notions, controlling and manipulative "learned" behaviors, negative attitude and poor outlook on life, harsh judgment received from society's standards of beauty, an extended single season or choosing to be Single by choice looked upon as a curse, biased gender roles and responsibilities, and stereotypical prejudice and sexism just from being a woman of color.

In the words of Valorie Burton, it doesn't matter if the task is harder or takes longer for you to accomplish, as long as you put forth the effort and remain disciplined & consistent until you master your craft, you will be unstoppable!

SonKiss Affirmation:

I am Expecting the Unexpected by...

(Fill in the blank with your personal statement. Repeat aloud several times until you believe it and commit to it. Post the message on your wall or mirror.)

Chapter 6

F-Forgive and Be Set Free

"Let all bitterness and wrath and anger and clamor and slander be put away from you, along with all malice. Be kind to one another, tenderhearted, forgiving one another, as God in Christ forgave you."- Ephesians 4:31-32 (ESV)

Reflection Questions:
(1) What are you holding on to that needs to be removed so you can be forgiven and set free?
(2) After you have forgiven yourself and others, describe how your life has changed for the better?

Many of us in the United States believe we live in the land of the free. Yet how many of us are truly free? Can we even handle the pressure and ridicule we may endure if we allow ourselves to be ourselves authentically?

Sadly, many of us will continue to lead a double life (killing ourselves on the inside) doing everything that we can to fit in and be accepted by others on the outside. Freedom involves removing the mask, the facade, the make-up, the weave, the negative "I can't" mindset, no more hiding behind materialistic things we use to define our existence, the lies we keep feeding ourselves, the hidden motives, and agendas, placing blame on others instead of self, and the jealousy and envy we feel when we cannot deal with others who are doing what we really want to do but we do not have the courage to do.

Forgiveness is the ultimate sacrifice that can lead to the greatest reward of freedom. Freedom is release from all pain, hurt, guilt, shame, bitterness, jealousy, envy, strife, depression, anxiety, animosity, greed, shame, doubt, and all fears. God paid the price for all of our sins by sacrificing his son Jesus Christ on Calvary. There is no need for you to forfeit your freedom that you have been given as a gift from God.

Pray to God, choose to let it go, ask for his forgiveness of your sins, accept that he forgives you, forgive yourself and all others (no matter what sins they have committed against you), repent (involves a change in your heart and/or change in your actions), and bask in your Freedom. The place of freedom brings unspeakable joy, love, peace, happiness, contentment, and life fulfillment.

SonKiss Affirmation:
I will Forgive and Be Set Free by…

(Fill in the blank with your personal statement. Repeat aloud several times until you believe it and commit to it. Post the message on your wall or mirror.)

Chapter 7

G-Get Away from the Noise and Focus

"Seek the Lord and his strength; seek his presence continually."- Psalms 105:4 (ESV)

Reflection Question:
 (1) How do you spend time in worship with God?

The safest place that exists is in the presence of the Lord. Women of Color must not allow the many distractions such as people (including family), television, radio, computers, phones, life accomplishments or hardships, and even ourselves (yes you and me) to get in the way of our quality time spent with our Savior Christ. We must learn to incorporate necessary mental breaks and praise moments to focus on the things of God that truly matter including our relationship with Him, our relationship with ourselves, and our relationship with others.

 Life is about learning how to balance each day. I enjoy being creative with my worship time including reading the scriptures, talking to God (both out loud and quietly depending on my location) in the morning or evening (nothing too formal, just honest conversation about what is on my heart), bible studies with friends or family at church, in the home, or on the phone, during lunch break, reading and posting scriptures all throughout the house (mirrors, refrigerator, desks, etc.), and my favorite is singing or praising in my car while stuck in traffic.

Then there are those times when we must simply be still, embrace silence, get away from everything, and totally give all focus to what God is saying and doing in your life. God is always available so you can choose the best place and time that works for you but worship time must be scheduled and completed daily.

The more time invested in praise and worship, the more power and victory are guaranteed. When we neglect our time spent with God, our lives become imbalanced and we slowly become overtaken by the heaviness and stress of the world. We start off feeling strong and fool ourselves into thinking that we can handle everything on our own. We slowly lose sight of God and life begins to erode and become meaningless and purposeless. Sadly, some of us lose all hope, fall into the enemy's trap of guilt, shame, and blame, and ultimately quit on life completely. It is in these moments that we must fall to our knees, repent, renew our mindset on things of God, continually seek His presence, and return to the word.

Calmly relax, focus all energy on receiving from God, listen to what He is saying, and do as He instructs when instructed and exactly how He instructed. Avoid delay or making changes on your own. Continue to seek Him if you misunderstand or need further assistance.

The message received may arrive in many different forms including a dream or mental image in your head, hearing a word from a person or on the radio or television (confirmation is received by hearing the same message over and over again), or God may speak a word or message directly to you (they will just naturally come to your mind). We can rest assured that we received the message from God because it yields peace in our hearts and minds. God is all powerful and can do the impossible!

SonKiss Affirmation:
I will continually seek God in worship by…

(Fill in the blank with your personal statement. Repeat aloud several times until you believe it and commit to it. Post the message on your wall or mirror.)

Chapter 8

H-Choose Life (Health) or Die Trying

Behold, I will bring to it health and healing, and I will heal them and reveal to them abundance of prosperity and security. "Jeremiah 33:6 (ESV)

Reflection Questions:
   (1) What lifestyle changes are you committing to do in order to be healthy and whole?
   (2) What actions are you committing to do or change to put yourselves first?

Women of color, we must be discipline to lead a life of health and healing. The enemy is very slick and cunning as he is able to make us believe that we are healthy if we simply look and feel healthy. Wrong!

Disease comes in many forms and may be disguised as "feeling normal or feeling good," having no symptoms to signal a problem, our ignorance, denial, or delay in dealing with little issues that come and go, lacking proper nutrition and exercise based on inflexible schedules or simply being lazy (we fail to see the significance of maintaining our health as a priority), and choosing to do wrong (making unhealthy choices, habits, or decisions) when you have been enlightened on how to choose and live a healthy lifestyle which in essence is willful sin. Women of color must nurture and develop our bodies: Physically (involves routine exercise recommended by your physician or maintaining activity as tolerated), and mentally (continually stimulate your brain by listening to music, reading books, etc.)

Emotionally (allow yourself to be vulnerable and cry, fall in love, journal/write, deal with your pain, face your fears, and verbalize your frustrations), and spiritually (connecting with our Heavenly Father for restoration and revival). Our ancestors did not have the pleasure of Google and so many other resources available to us.

We have NO EXCUSE! We must choose health or die trying. We must empower ourselves by gaining and applying healthy wisdom (only from trusted resources and websites). We must be willing to move beyond the normal: shop around, sample, and cook different types of healthy foods, research creative ways to be fit, and connect with likeminded healthy people who can support us in our journey.

We must become the expert on our bodies and do what our bodies' need to sustain life.

We must be willing to experience trial and error until we have mastered the workings of our bodies. We must learn to keep what works and get rid of what does not work. Maintaining balance is always key (too much or too little of something over time can lead to damage). ***Women of color must choose life by taking care of themselves first!***

On every flight before take-off, we are instructed in the event of an emergency, we must first place the oxygen mask on us first and then assist our family. Women of color have been conditioned to take care of everyone and everything before ourselves. This negative mindset and stereotypical typecast must end now.

Women of Color First Pledge:

"We are no longer bound by the role of playing not good enough, not enough, second best, almost, not quite there yet, least, and last in line. We are in first place and are leaving those things far behind. We are honored to be called sisters, wives, mothers, aunts, grandmothers, god-mothers, step-mothers, and adoptive-mothers, however, we will put ourselves 1st! We will keep ourselves (second to God and husband, if applicable) as a top priority and take optimal care of our bodies, our hearts, our minds, our assets, our goals, our dreams, our aspirations, and our lives as a whole. We will invest in doing the things necessary (eating healthy, exercising, working, resting, relaxing, giving, and maintaining balance in our lives) to keep us healthy and whole. We possess beauty and boldness and will allow nothing and no one to stop us from victory in Christ Jesus. We matter and we will never apologize for being our best selves."

SonKiss Affirmation:

I will Choose Health and put myself first by…

(Fill in the blank with your personal statement. Repeat aloud several times until you believe it and commit to it. Post the message on your wall or mirror.)

Chapter 9

I-Invest in Yourself

"Do your best to present yourself to God as one approved, a worker who has no need to be ashamed, rightly handling the word of truth."
-II Timothy 2:15 (ESV)

Reflection Questions:
    (1) What must I start or stop doing to become my best self? (2) How? (3) When?

Women of color must choose to make the ultimate sacrifice and commit to Investing in You! Investing in oneself is never selfish. It is how we learn to love, honor, and respect our greatest asset: ourselves. This process involves ongoing creating, innovating, sharpening your skills, pruning, detoxing, and letting go of what is not good for you, what is not right for you, what is stealing your peace and your health and learning to adopt and embrace the mindset and value of finding what is best for me, what is helping me, what is healing me, what is keeping me safe, and what is helping me to grow and prosper.

    Like a naive fool, I kept waiting on others to put in a good word, a favor, a prayer, or a few extra dollars as "they" promised. It was either a lie, scam, or someone expecting some type of favor or something in return. I can count on one hand the number of individuals who honored their word. I finally reached a point where I got tired of all the betrayal and I decided, I can and will do it myself. I must be willing to give my all to receive my all. I also learned to watch others who already had achieved what I desired and to use their experiences (achievements and lessons) to my advantage.

Stop asking others for permission. Stop apologizing for your success. Stop procrastinating and eliminate those patterns of self-sabotage because you are fearful of success.

You are deserving and worthy of all that God has in store for you BUT YOU MUST DO THE WORK!!! There are no shortcuts. Commit to do ALL you can do to become the BEST YOU (study, practice, read, write, sing, dance, or do whatever it takes until you master your craft) on a daily basis. It is wise to become an expert in a particular subject area rather than to spread yourself too thinly or be willing to pay a trusted connoisseur to work on your behalf (In essence, become the best or invest in the best).

In most cases, people are hired based on the "perceived" value and significance they bring to the table. You must always present your best self (right attire, right words, and knowing the right way to perform…in a sense). Here's a little secret no one will tell you: In many jobs, you are not hired solely based on your previous experience but on your ability to think, speak, and act with competence and confidence under pressure.

The skillsets can always be learned but can your personality shine under pressure or will you be easily broken, offended, or lash out? Are you able to be consistent in looking and acting the part or following the script you have been given? The actual training is not in orientation but is "learned on the job."

Thus, maintaining a lifestyle of planning and preparation is a necessity for women of color. Prior to accepting any position, please complete your research in advance and learn what you are potentially signing up for. Is this right for you? Is this position in right alignment with your personal values and beliefs? Is working for someone else best for you or would you work better at being your own boss?

And, if you choose to be your own boss, are you disciplined to do what it takes to survive as the boss? Women of color are expected to be better, to know more, and do more with less. And remember, you have the option to peacefully walk away if something is not right for you. Always do what is best for you!

SonKiss Affirmation:
I will invest in myself by...

(Fill in the blank with your personal statement. Repeat aloud several times until you believe it and commit to it. Post the message on your wall or mirror.)

Chapter 10

J-Journey into Unknown Territory

"Behold, I will do a new thing; now it springs forth, do you not perceive it? I will make a way in the wilderness and rivers in the desert."
- Isaiah 43:19 (ESV)

Reflection Questions:
  (1) Have you ever considered that your way of thinking, seeing, and overall living is all wrong?
  (2) What if someone asked you to consider changing your entire existence or vicariously living like someone completely different from you?
  (3) What would your life consist of if you were born another sex or race, reared in a different country, or spoke another language?

Women of color must be bold, brave, and willing to stretch their wings into the unknown. This is the only way for us to gain new momentum and is a necessity for us to beat the odds (however insurmountable) ensuring we remain extraordinary. Each new generation will call for a new level of excellence to be reached in order for us to reign as the true champions we have always been.

A generation that fails to meet our standard of excellence becomes cursed and begins a cycle of mediocrity and our rich heritage and legacy of greatness slowly disappears as if it never existed.

Life would seem so "uncommon" and not your usual normal experience. It would seem scary at first and very intimidating. As your fellow woman of color with similar experiences, I challenge you to be "uncommon" in the common world. To become "uncommon", we must choose to journey into unknown territory which include being open and receptive to challenges, taking risks, and doing things that are uncomfortable and difficult.

Women of color: I encourage you to get away from the television and read all kinds of books, spend money on seeing the world (travel internationally) and new experiences rather than spending on material possessions, and instead of following the same boring routine, spice up your life by exploring new interests specifically the things you said you would never do. In most cases, we may be fearful based on negative childhood experiences that robbed us of our confidence.

Refuse to allow your insecurities, past hurts, and failures to block your future of freedom and possibilities. Pray, use caution, and go for it! Your life will never be the same again!

Make a list of the new experiences and challenges you plan to do each year including the date and friends you will invite to join you.

Write it below.

SonKiss Affirmation:
I will Journey into the unknown by…

(Fill in the blank with your personal statement. Repeat aloud several times until you believe it and commit to it. Post the message on your wall or mirror.)

Chapter 11

K-Know Your Value

"Give, and it will be given to you. Good measure, pressed down, shaken together, running over, will be put into your lap. For with the measure you use it will be measured back to you."-Luke 6:38 (ESV)

Reflection Questions:

(1) How can your personal life lessons help you to discover your "hidden value?"
(2) What do you feel is your purpose or hidden value?

Women of Color are much like rare gems hidden beneath the earth's surface waiting to be discovered. Maybe you're a dazzling diamond, a sophisticated sapphire, a radiant ruby, or an elegant emerald like me? Where is your value?

Where do you shine, and come alive? Have you discovered your "hidden value" or the reason why you were created? Do you realize how loved, appreciated, and valued you are by your Heavenly Father? Your unique purpose is directly connected to the value you possess. Everything in your life has meaning and value (your skills, talents, abilities, experiences, and weaknesses).

My motto is to use all that I have in giving and serving others wholeheartedly as if giving to God. I was created in the image and likeness of Christ to use the value earned from my life experiences to bring enlightenment and empowerment to my fellow sisters in Christ.

My purpose is to add value by teaching women who look like me to discover and treasure their value and self-worth. People will invest in you because of the value you can bring to them. Find out what the client or customer wants, execute, and deliver, and always make the client or customer feel significant.

This can only be done if you first know your value and charge for what you are worth. (If you struggle with feeling valued, I encourage you to spend time reading, reciting out loud, and memorizing the word of God until your value is completely restored and focus on getting you in right alignment with God.

This is not the time to pursue other relationships because others may unintentionally feed off of your insecurity and not give you the value you truly deserve). Ministry and/or business is never free of charge.

There is always a cost when you are pouring out your gifts. Discounts are nice but they have the potential to lower your value. Once your value is lowered, people may lose respect and feel a sense of false entitlement that you do not deserve what you are really worth. If someone cannot respect the value that you bring (personally and/or professionally), it is wise to keep it moving and not waste your time. You are worth more! God always has greater in store.

SonKiss Affirmation:
I will add value to my life by …

(Fill in the blank with your personal statement. Repeat aloud several times until you believe it and commit to it. Post the message on your wall or mirror.)

Chapter 12

L-Live Life on Your Terms

"The thief comes to steal, kill, and destroy. But I have come that you might have life abundantly." -John 10:10 (ESV)

Reflection Questions:

    (1) What are some of the ways you can "live life on your terms?"

    (2) By doing what, with whom, how, when?

I'm pretty certain that at this point, you're probably thinking I'm coming off sounding extremely selfish. However, I am simply enlightening you that your dreams, goals, plans, and priorities should always remain relevant and a focal point for you.

We as women of color are bombarded with every distraction known to man (family matters, health issues, money problems, etc.) and it's very easy to lose yourself by putting what matters to you on the backburner for another time or another season in the future. Sorry to inform you that life always brings new drama as the time passes. Now is the perfect time to go back to school, purchase your dream home, travel, and see the world, write, and publish your novel, start your own business, or choose a healthier lifestyle.

Whatever you are envisioning as your biggest dreams and aspirations, aspire to turn them into your realities in this lifetime.

Tomorrow may be too late and you may never reach retirement. Many have become terminally ill or have passed away without getting a chance to live and enjoy the life they desired.

They settled and lived mediocre while focusing on living paycheck to paycheck (just trying to make it mentality) or allowed others to enjoy the fruit of their labor. They were merely existing and not really living. Let us avoid living with regret by choosing to live life to the fullest now.

What does this mean? We will find what works best for us and Live Life on our Terms.

We will never settle for less than Gods' best.

We will create a way when there is no way. We will make our own rules. We will seek and find ways to maintain a balanced and healthy life. We will think outside of the box. We will leverage our strengths. We will learn to say no to others and yes to ourselves. We will set the tone to show others how we expect to be treated. We will keep the right perspective while keeping our peace. We will master our communication skills by learning what to say, how to say it, saying only what is necessary without oversharing, when to say it, and how to purposely use silence.

We will be receptive to discipline and correction and will enforce discipline and correction when applicable. We will set aside time each day to reflect on what is most important to us. We will be accountable to ourselves. We will assign a trusted Accountability Sister to help us reach our goals, if needed. We will be accountable to other Women of Color. We will hold others accountable to their word.

SonKiss Affirmation:
I choose to Live Life on my Terms by …

(Fill in the blank with your personal statement. Repeat aloud several times until you believe it and commit to it. Post the message on your wall or mirror.)

Chapter 13

G-Goodbye Mediocrity, Hello Mastermind

"I can do all things through Christ who strengthens me."- Phil. 4:13 (ESV)

Reflection Questions:
(1) What are you allowing to keep you in a place of mediocrity?
(2) How can you envision your life as a Mastermind? What do you see?

It's time for us to give a swift kick in the butt to mediocrity and open our eyes, ears, and hearts to a brand new mastermind: "I Can Do All Things through Christ" mentality. Women of color must engage, connect, fellowship, and network with the elite, the top dogs, the movers and shakers, and the game changers who are transforming our lives for the better. Here are the 7 steps required to move from mediocrity to mastermind:

Step 1: Release the Lack Mentality by:

a. Complete a self-evaluation of your beliefs, patterns, behaviors, thoughts, actions, etc. that are connected to anything you "think" you lack. Why do I think and act the way I do? Where did this originate from?

b. Based on your findings in bullet "a," determine if it is not healthy or productive that you will let it go.

c. Invest in learning ways to live in abundance and freedom. How can I change my thinking and actions to lead to successful outcomes? Commit to making changes that are possible and dealing with and making peace with past mistakes that cannot be erased or changed.

d. Request another associate or colleague to give you honest feedback about you (select someone who can be impartial and unbiased, family and close friends not included). Listen to understand how others perceive you and focus on improvements, if applicable.

e. Become the "subject matter expert" in your line of business.

Step 2: Create the "Master Plan" by:

a. Seeking the Heavenly Master for instructions and guidance.

b. Observe, listen, and learn from the Elite who have already paved the way (no need to re-invent the wheel). Simply make tweaks and changes that are unique to your business model.

Step 3: Write the Plan to Right the Plan. It doesn't become real or the right plan until it's placed on paper and you can see it with your own eyes.

   a. Create your unique and catchy "Elevator Pitch."
   b. Be impeccable with your words.
   c. Choose your personal "Theme Song" that will keep you focused and motivated. Play it regularly.

Step 4: Execute and Deliver your "Master Plan" (make no delay).

Step 5: Evaluate your outcomes based on results achieved. Afterwards, re-evaluate and make changes based on what you discover works best for you.

Step 6: Continue this ongoing cycle of productivity 24/7 while simultaneously growing your skills and abilities to steadily increase your net worth.

Step 7: Share your story with others who aspire to become a Mastermind. Be mindful to protect your name and brand (in advance). Allow no one to take credit for or steal your work. Seek legal counsel or hire an attorney if needed.

SonKiss Affirmation:

I will become a Mastermind by...
(Fill in the blank with your personal statement. Repeat aloud several times until you believe it and commit to it. Post the message on your wall or mirror.)

Chapter 14

N-The Necessity of Structure

"A slack hand causes poverty, but the hand of the diligent makes rich."-Proverbs 10:4 (ESV) "The plans of the diligent lead surely to abundance, but everyone who is hasty comes only to poverty."-Proverbs 21:5

Reflection Questions:
(1) What are the areas in your life in need of structure?
(2) What is your plan of action to gain structure? How will you achieve this plan?
(3) Who and what is best for us in this season?
(4) What tasks must be done to reach our destiny?
(5) What must we stop doing immediately to begin seeing results?
(6) Who must we keep in our lives and who must go?
(7) How must we structure our daily lives to be successful?

Women of color need structure to be productive! In my opinion and based on my experiences, Structure involves many aspects of our lives including timing/punctuality, organization, priority management, and proper positioning and alignment.

We require structure in our health, finances, work and play time, choices and decisions, career, and life purpose, and in our home and our hearts. Structure is needed to protect you and your assets. In my own personal life, my need for structure was extremely difficult and it involved me repeating the same cycles (starting, stopping, starting over, moving forward with some progress, then getting pushed back further, and starting over again) and problems (health issues, failed relationships, missed opportunities, debt, and debt collectors, dealing with con artists, and get rich quick scams) until I decided to **fully commit** to produce.

The pain of remaining the same became so great that I just couldn't take it anymore. I had no choice but to grow up and re-commit to God and myself in becoming this new-and improved me.

This structure change was quite unbearable in the beginning but it became easier as I vowed to be productive by "doing something" every day. Even if I only reached a small level of success, it gave me the will power needed to keep "doing something" every day. I had to give up sleeping in on the weekends, frivolous shopping on things that depreciate or lose value over time, many unhealthy and tasty foods, many nights of television, minimizing time spent on social media, and many hours of time hanging out with friends before I became productive.

I later realized that I was causing self-sabotage and delayed obedience by the distractions mentioned above. Here is the blueprint of how I chose to structure my life for success: I made a choice to get up early every day before sunrise to pray and spend time with God, stretch my entire body, write out my daily to-do list, work on my business before working on my 95, invest in reading books and taking new courses, researching and discovering healthy foods and healthy food chains, finding creative ways to be active and enjoy the outdoors on a regular basis, and becoming wise in utilizing both my time and money with purpose.

Productivity is the by-product of self-discipline, setting clear and concise goals, setting and maintaining boundaries, keeping the right priorities, consistent follow-through, and most importantly being obedient following God's Will for our lives. It involves ongoing planning, preparation, and making power (faith) moves as lead by God.

Everyone and everything has a divine place and order and we must master: the who, what, when, where, why, and how that will maximize our daily productivity leading to optimal results. Structure is the prerequisite to Productivity

SonKiss Affirmation:
I will Structure my life by…

(Fill in the blank with your personal statement. Repeat aloud several times until you believe it and commit to it. Post the message on your wall or mirror.)

Chapter 15

O- Be Slow to Take Offense

"Know this, my beloved brothers: let every person be quick to hear, slow to speak, and slow to anger; for the anger of man does not produce the righteousness of God." James 1:19-20 (ESV)

Reflection Questions:
(1) How can our lives be positively impacted by being slow to take offense?
(2) What are the benefits of being slow to take offense?

We, as women of color must stop taking everything so personal. I understand how unfair this may seem because I struggled with this issue for years. I kept internalizing and overanalyzing everything that was happening to me and getting my feelings hurt. I chose to mentally accept and take on both positive and negative thoughts or emotions that landed in my head.

Thus, I felt I had a right to be angry, depressed, and many times lash out verbally or physically when others would hate on me for no reason at all. I created this protective wall and it became almost impossible to trust, allow myself to accept love, and love others. There are also times when trusted family members or friends may (unintentionally) verbally attack you or attempt to transfer negative energy towards you.

Sometimes our family members and friends choose to take out their frustrations on the ones who are closest to them when they are not aware of how to properly deal with and manage their emotions in a constructive manner. This may occur if our family members or friends feel humiliated, stressed out, sleep deprived, physically or mentally drained, or overwhelmed.

We, as women of color, must learn and be able to recognize these symptoms, use effective communication techniques that allow us to acknowledge and confront the issue in the moment, respond in love without being offended (or holding on to the offense), release the issue and let it go, and forgive ourselves and others for all of our mistakes (as soon as possible) as this internal pain will eat away at us and which can potentially lead to sickness.

It is very difficult to process at that time but the reality is "It's Not About You" but rather about what "that person" is internally or externally dealing with. You do not have to accept ownership of someone else's unresolved issues.

Women of color can pick and choose the thoughts they wish to think on. Choose your thoughts wisely as they will determine your actions which will determine how successful you can become.

Women of color are not "angry or bitter" as we are commonly portrayed in the media and we must live in a manner that represents our true worth and value as daughters of a Heavenly King. Our daily living should represent the fruit of the spirit: love, joy, peace, patience, kindness, goodness, faithfulness, gentleness, and self-control. Stop pretending as if you know it all and let others help you when needed. Remove that humongous chip off of your shoulder.

Learn to control your response to difficult challenges and/or negative stimuli that are promised to come your way and not allow these challenges or negativity to control you.

First of all, you must be willing to determine what are you allowing or have allowed in your spirit that angers, hurts, or manipulates you in negative way and discover how to remove these things immediately.

Your success will be a turn off for many who secretly hate you and their main intent is to attack you or distract you. They are offended by your courage and tenacity to live your dreams. This is more incentive for you to keep moving forward (while they continue to hate) and pray for their healing. Be mindful of predators who will use secrecy, prolonged silence, and partial truths to blind you from the whole truth. There are many wolves lurking around in sheep's clothing who have learned how to masquerade as sheep and do it quite well. Over time, they reveal their true identity because they always return to who they really are. Pay close attention to patterns and ensure actions match words consistently on a long – term basis. In many instances, people will covertly or secretly plot and scheme to get under your skin by saying and doing things that will piss you off or tarnish your name and character. They are trying to get a negative reaction from you. Never give them the satisfaction! We must remember that God will always show up and show out by providing a "Godly Response Strategy"!

Here is your **Godly Response Strategy**:

Step 1: Listen to your spirit of discernment by recognizing the attack (hidden or in plain sight). You will normally get a "feeling that something just is not right" on the inside. Do not ignore these feelings.

Step 2: Choose to defuse the situation by maintaining professionalism (reduce the danger, calm the situation). Determine if a response is necessary (may or may not be). Silence may be warranted. If a response is needed, ensure your words and demeanor are focused on resolution via factual information only and address the issue (not the person). Avoid making any personal judgment against the person. Seek a higher authority in dealing with the person.

Step 3: Keep the right perspective at all times. Use each experience as a life tool sent from God to make you better. Make a decision that you will refuse to be offended by rejection and ridicule and focus your energy on allowing the lesson to revamp and prepare you for future life lessons.

SonKiss Affirmation:
I will commit to be slow to take offense by...

(Fill in the blank with your personal statement. Repeat aloud several times until you believe it and commit to it. Post the message on your wall or mirror.)

Chapter 16

P- Purge (Rid) & Purify (Cleanse) Your Temple

"Create in me a clean heart O God, and renew a right spirit within me." -Psalms 51:10 (ESV)

Reflection Questions:
> (1) Why is it important to purge and purify your temple?

The word of God is always available to help you purge and purify your temple. God never created a designated place inside your temple for: anger, animosity, baggage, depression, doubt, envy, fear, greed, guilt, insecurity, jealousy, lust, pride, self -hate, or shame to reside.

You are no longer stuck playing the host to these elements of infection that slowly eat away and destroy your inner beauty and soul and cause you to lose your immunity (covering and protection) in Christ Jesus.

Your temple also includes your personal living space and the people & surroundings you keep. It is wise to maintain organization and cleanliness as you are rewarded a sense of internal peace and contentment when you can easily see, appreciate, and enjoy all God has given to you.

Many times we have collected so much "stuff" that we lose ourselves by getting attached to things and "clutter" takes away from our focus. Stuff and clutter eventually lead to distraction, procrastination, and corrupt our thinking causing us to make bad or delayed decisions.

Other times we become connected to the wrong people without even knowing until it's too late. Thus, routine cleaning on a regular basis is key by ridding your space of old, outdated, or unused items and removing people who no longer serve a purpose or their season in your life has ended.

Many will do what is called "spring cleaning" but I encourage you to purge, and purify daily, weekly, monthly, or annually as needed. Getting essential sleep (rest) is also essential in being renewed as it allows your brain to function properly which causes us our bodies to work properly.

Purge and Purify by:
1. Reading and obeying the word of God consistently.
2. Routinely self-examining our lives for areas where we struggle and taking ownership to resolve our issues.
3. Removing people and things that no longer serve our purpose.
4. Re-writing the script for our lives by living according to the word of God (actively praying and receiving healing and deliverance, maintaining a healthy lifestyle by making better choices, etc.)
5. Rest and renewal on a daily basis.

SonKiss Affirmation:
I will Purge and/or Purify my life by…

(Fill in the blank with your personal statement. Repeat aloud several times until you believe it and commit to it. Post the message on your wall or mirror.)

Chapter 17

Q- Ask the Right Questions the Right Way

"Do not be anxious about anything, but in everything by prayer and supplication with thanksgiving let your requests be made known to God. And the peace of God, which surpasses all understanding, will guard your hearts and your minds in Christ Jesus."
- Philippians 4:6-8 (ESV)

Reflection Question:

> (1) What are you doing to enhance your speaking and presentation skills?

Many relationships fail because we are inadequately equipped in our communication and presentation skills which causes us to lose the girl or guy of our dreams, are overlooked for the promotion, and/or misinterpret what was seen or heard (from our lack of understanding).

Thus, women of color must learn to ask the right questions the right way! We must properly structure the content of our questions to receive the desired outcome. Our questions should be open-ended (allowing the other person to elaborate and give detail) or closed ended (when we desire a simple yes or no reply).

Both open-ended questions and closed ended questions are necessary in a healthy conversation. We should ensure our questions are clear, specific, and purposeful. What will get you the "buy in" from your customer? If you do not understand what is being said, reflect by saying "so what you are saying is" to clarify you "got the message" so you can respond correctly. Before we can ask the right questions, we must first enhance our speaking and presentation skills through coaching, training, mentoring, and ongoing practice which will give us confidence in learning the best way to master asking the right questions the right way. Practice by speaking consistently in front of others, standing in front of a mirror, learning from your own mistakes, and from observing the mistakes of others.

Your speaking voice (clear and easily audible, not too loud or soft), speed of your words (typically match the speed of the other speaker), diversity in vocabulary, ability to stay focused on the subject matter, maintain timely delivery, good eye contact, and remembering smiling and laughter (when applicable) all work together in proper delivery of the right questions the right way and the feedback received.

We must also learn the right way to talk to God. We should always seek God from a place of reverence, giving Him all the honor, praise, and glory due to Him, thanking Him for who He is and for all He has done and continues to do, and speak to Him as if speaking to a tender-hearted, loving, and caring parent who loves us unconditionally which includes discipline and correcting us when needed.

We can let down our guards, speak from the heart being honest with Him, repent of our sins, and bask in his presence giving Him our full attention.

SonKiss Affirmation:
I will Ask the Right Questions the Right Way by …

(Fill in the blank with your personal statement. Repeat aloud several times until you believe it and commit to it. Post the message on your wall or mirror.)

Chapter 18

R- Resilience Is in Our Nature

"As it is written, "For your sake we are being killed all the day long; we are regarded as sheep to be slaughtered." No, in all these things we are more than conquerors through Him who loves us."- Romans 8: 36-37 (ESV)

Reflection Question:
    (1) Describe the ways in which you can be resilient or bounce back when you fall down.

Women of color have historically had the greatest level of resilience also known as "bounce back power." We have fallen and always found a way to bounce back from the days of slavery, the Great Depression, the Reconstruction period, while fighting for the 19th amendment giving women the right to vote in 1920 (although many African American women in the South did not have the right to vote until many decades later), the Civil Rights Era, and from the Afrocentric 70s all the way to the reign of our current woman of color, our former First Lady Michelle Obama.

We have no choice but to survive and be great because it is in our genetic make-up. We are very similar to the palm tree as God gave us the ability to bend forwards and backwards during tough winds as we are unbreakable by the power of the Holy Spirit within us. Women of color are those in the same because so many of our ancestors were sold and separated via slave trade. We are truly our sister's keeper and must strive to maintain unity, peace, and love among each other whether we are blood related or solely related by the melanin in our skin.

Although you may never receive the recognition and accolades for leading this sisterhood, other women of color are counting on you to get up, step up, and speak up. They are cheering you on behind the scenes because you look like them, act like them, think like them, have a mother or father who looks like them, were raised with similar values like them, are attacked and demeaned like them, hurt like them, cry like them, and when you win, they win.

Women of Color are leaving a huge impact by imparting wisdom to other women of color to be bold, courageous, and step out on Faith to live the life of your dreams. Whenever I am feeling low, I choose to think on the sacrifices of my ancestors who were enslaved, raped, beaten, tortured, and in the midst of it all, they never gave up. They worked in excellence and maintained their homes and family making the best of what they had even if it was not much. Neither of my parents received a high school education (they dropped out being forced to work and help support their families), however, I am a college graduate who was highly encouraged by them that I could achieve anything with an education and to make the most of my life.

Even when I failed and lost my scholarship, my parents refused to let me quit or give up. They made a way for me to know and fear God, instill values to invest in myself and empower others, appreciate my blessings no matter how big or how small, make lifestyle changes to break generational curses, and leave a legacy for future generations to come.

This book is just the beginning of my legacy. Thus, I can never give up on my fellow beautiful and gifted women of color who look like me. We will rise!

SonKiss Affirmation:
I will be Resilient by …

(Fill in the blank with your personal statement. Repeat aloud several times until you believe it and commit to it. Post the message on your wall or mirror.)

Chapter 19

S- OutSHINE the Competition

"Whatever you do, work heartily, as for the Lord and not for men, knowing that from the Lord you will receive the inheritance as your reward. You are serving the Lord Christ."
- Colossians 3:23-24 (ESV)

Reflection Question:
(1) How will you as a Woman of Color OutSHINE the competition?

Serena and Venus Williams, Laila Ali, Queen Latifah, Beyoncé, Eartha Kitt, Dorothy Dandridge, Whitney Houston, Lena Horne, Florence Griffith-Joyner, Jennifer Lopez, Lucy Liu, Eva Mendes, Frieda Pinto and Gabby Douglas all have a few things in common. They are all beautiful and talented women of color who have beat the odds in sports, music, and film and television. Each has proved that "all things are possible through Christ" with tremendous high work ethic, perseverance, and faith to believe and stay the course until you receive it.

They accepted NO EXCUSES and neither should we. **Women of color must commit to discipline, diligence, dedication, and a desire to wholeheartedly serve our Lord and Savior Christ**

in ALL that we say and do. Our daily living should be example and message of a life of love, grace, mercy, favor, and daily dying to self. We are not given the same advantages as other races. Based on my personal experiences,

I feel women of color must commit to work three times harder (personally and professionally) in order to OutSHINE the competition. We must choose to work when others are sleeping and partying. But the real secret is that our biggest competition is… ourselves! We must continually test and re-test ourselves as we OutSHINE our former (old) person by taking on new opportunities (usually disguised as problems).

Let's examine the three similarities of how women of color can OutSHINE the competition by using Jesus Christ as an example:

1. We have been saved or set apart by receiving Jesus Christ as our Lord and Savior. To OutSHINE the competition, you must be **set apart** and be received as different and uncommon. Your high work ethic will set you apart from others who are not as driven and accountable as you.

2. Jesus Christ stood out from the crowd and left a memory on the many lives that were touched, saved, and healed by Him. To OutSHINE the Competition, you must possess the "wow factor" to **stand out** and leave an

unforgettable memory that captivates the hearts and minds of your audience for a lifetime.

3. Jesus Christ possessed the ability to **stay the course** by dying on calvary for all our sins. To OutSHINE the competition, quitting is never an option no matter how many delays, denials, or difficulties we must face. We must stay the course until we reach our destiny.

SonKiss Affirmation:
I will OutSHINE the Competition by ...

(Fill in the blank with your personal statement. Repeat aloud several times until you believe it and commit to it. Post the message on your wall or mirror.)

Chapter 20

T- Treat You with Tender Loving Care

"After all, no one ever hated his own body, but he feeds and cares for it, just as Christ does the church, for we are members of his body."
-Ephesians 5: 29-30 (NIV)

Reflection Question:
(1) In what ways are choosing to "Treat You with Tender Loving Care"?

As women of color we must continually practice loving ourselves unconditionally and giving ourselves the best because we are worth it! Jesus is our best example of our Tender Lover and we must model our love language after Him. Loving ourselves and keeping ourselves as a priority is not a selfish act but rather an act of self-love which is vital for our well-being. The act of loving involves many facets including:

1. Self-respect and respect for others
   a. Be mindful of the way you carry yourself at all times (attire, attitude, actions, and words should reflect Godly character).
   b. Be authentic and freely express who you are.
2. Taking care of your physical health

    a. Investing in eating healthy foods
    b. Maintaining regular daily activity,
    c. creating a specific exercise routine approved by your physician, or
    d. obtaining a personal trainer if needed
    e. Getting adequate rest
3. Taking care of your mental; emotional; and spiritual health
    a. Daily study and devotional time with God (I recommend setting aside at least 15-30 minutes at the same time each day and starting a journal to gather your thoughts).
    b. Committing to being a life learner (continually study new courses, read books, and invest in new opportunities for personal and professional development).
    c. Foster new relationships via networking and being socially active.
    d. Giving and/or serving on a regular basis.
4. Financial Empowerment
    a. Educate yourself on ways to build and maintain financial freedom (saving, investing, budgeting, and using credit to your advantage).
    b. Invest in a financial expert if needed.

5. Grooming
   a. Routine maintenance of skin, hair, face, hands, nails, and feet.
   b. Women of color must ROCK CONFIDENCE!
6. Rewards are required
   a. Treat yourself on a regular basis as you choose by shopping, traveling, massage therapy, eating delicious food treats, etc.

SonKiss Affirmation:
I will Treat myself with Tender Loving Care by …

(Fill in the blank with your personal statement. Repeat aloud several times until you believe it and commit to it. Post the message on your wall or mirror.)

Chapter 21

U- Lift Up the (Godly) Standard

"You are the light of the world. A city set on a hill cannot be hidden. Nor do people light a lamp and put it under a basket, but on a stand, and it gives light to all in the house. In the same way, let your light shine before others, so that they may see your good works and give glory to your Father who is in heaven."
- Matthew 5: 14-16 (ESV)

Reflection Question:
   (1) As a woman of color, in what ways will you lift up the godly standard of excellence?

Jesus Christ is our greatest example of our standard of excellence or greatness. My parents were the "physical manifestation of Jesus" that I saw while growing up in the South. My father displayed excellence via consistency and follow through by working Monday through Saturday and attending church every Sunday.

My mother displayed excellence via discipline by overseeing duties as wife and mother including working, cooking, cleaning, budgeting, and paying bills on time all while rearing eight children and three grandchildren alongside my father.

I may not have always had name brands or many choices but I never experienced a day without food, clothing, or shelter. From a very early age, my parents instilled godly standards and values including reverencing the one true God our sovereign Lord and Savior Jesus Christ and following His commandments, living a lifestyle of serving and giving representing the character of Christ, respecting our elders and each other, avoiding being wasteful by using all you have, making the most of every moment and every experience (positive and negative), choosing health and wealth as priorities, having zero tolerance for any form of disrespect or abuse, speaking and standing up for what you believe in, teaching that forgiveness is a necessity in healing including forgiving yourself, recognizing that life is a balancing act of learning how to effectively manage work and play, and living and enjoying life to the fullest!

Women of color are called to lift up one another and exude a standard of excellence in our daily living. We are the role models of our fellow sisters and brothers, and we must let our godly example shine and continue the legacy of godly character and transformation to a world being hypnotized by the many (temporary and carnal) pleasures that will lead to sin and eventually death. It is normal that your experiences may vary greatly from mine.

However, the godly principles and impact should remain the same as we serve the same God.

SonKiss Affirmation:
I will Let My Light Shine by …

(Fill in the blank with your personal statement. Repeat aloud several times until you believe it and commit to it. Post the message on your wall or mirror.)

Chapter 22

V- Victim to Visionary Mind Shift

"Finally, brothers and sisters, whatever is true, whatever is noble, whatever is right, whatever is pure, whatever is lovely, whatever is admirable, if anything is excellent or praiseworthy, think about such things." - Phil. 4:8 (NIV)

Reflection Question:
> (1) What is your plan of action to shift your mindset from victim to visionary?

One summer day I was listening to a song that reminded me of an old friend (let's call her Donna). It was her favorite song. As I listened to the song and reminisced about our memories together, I could see her beautiful smile and hear her soft voice adding in her own words when she didn't know the part of the song. Donna always had a way of making me feel good about myself. What is really crazy is that a few minutes later, I met up with my new friend Charlene. But, I realized I had said, "Hi Donna. How are you?"

Charlene looked puzzled for a moment and returned a huge smile and laughter. I was in shock because I couldn't believe I mixed up their names. Some would classify this error as a "Freudian Slip" but in reality, my subconscious mind was so consumed with positive thoughts of Donna that my mouth verbally expressed what I was thinking out loud. My hidden thoughts were exposed and brought to light.

Do you now realize how important it is to choose your thoughts wisely? We have the power (via the Holy Spirit) to choose or block the thoughts that enter our mind. Free your mind by focusing on the things of God!

I encourage every woman of color to choose to have a visionary mind shift and release the victim mentality! This victim mentality is filled with **choices** that are dangerous to our well-being including the following:

1. Making excuses for the things that have happened to us (beyond our control)
2. Playing the blame game including blaming God (it's nobody's fault)
3. Taking our frustrations and pain out on others who are closest to us
4. Choosing to inflict pain on ourselves
5. Accepting low or no Standards/maintaining a low self-esteem
6. Refusing to take responsibility for our actions
7. Refusing to face or deal with our unresolved issues

8. Carrying internal and/or external baggage weighing us down

9. Remaining stagnant or stuck when God is telling us to move, act, or make changes
10. Plotting evil and hate against our fellow sisters and brothers

Let's choose to be renewed to the visionary mind shift by doing the following (**always do what works for you**):

1. Choosing to think on the things of God (requires regular study of the word of God) by following these principles:
    a. Feed your mind and spirit with the word of God by allowing your eyes and ears to consistently receive the word of God by watching Christian programs on TV, purchasing Christian based books and paraphernalia, and listening to music and podcasts that focus on the word of God.
    b. Choose to reject negative thoughts and images that enter our head which may require us to avoid certain people, TV programs, social media sites, music, books, etc.

c. Write and/or memorize scriptures meaningful to you and recite them out aloud if the ungodly thoughts are extremely consuming.

d. Writing out your thoughts is another method of release as it allows the junk to leave your head and land on paper. Seeing it on paper may also help you to face it and deal with it.

e. Fasting and Praying are essential components of this process (follow the leading of the Holy Spirit).

2. Changing our perspective, words, and actions leading to health and wholeness (this involves a commitment to changing your life by focusing on loving Christ, self, and others in both good and bad circumstances. Forgiveness along with corrected action is key).

3. Creating a Vision Board and transferring these positive and Godinspired images from your mind to paper. See it with your spiritual eyes and physical eyes. Please be selective in sharing your visions as everyone cannot handle your vision. Turn your vision into your reality.

4. Serving, volunteering, or joining a ministry team willing to help others. Life becomes more bearable when we remove the focus from self to helping someone else. Ministry participation can also strengthen you in the word of God.

5. I recommend we strive to serve in our communities at least 1-2 times a year.

6. If these methods are unsuccessful, seeking counseling or therapy may be warranted. Although we are saved and historically therapy is seen as "taboo" in the church, we must be open to seeking professional help if life is getting the best of us. We owe it to ourselves to seek God's best for us.

SonKiss Affirmation:
I will choose a Visionary Mindset by …

(Fill in the blank with your personal statement. Repeat aloud several times until you believe it and commit to it. Post the message on your wall or mirror.)

Chapter 23

W- Woman Up (Building Up Your Sisters in Christ)

"So Christ himself gave the apostles, the prophets, the evangelists, the pastors, and teachers, to equip his people for works of service, so that the body of Christ may be built up until we all reach unity in the faith and in the knowledge of the Son of God and become mature, attaining to the whole measure of the fullness of Christ." -Ephesians 4: 11-13 (NIV)

Reflection Question:
(1) Describe different examples of how we as women of color cam build up each other? By doing what?

We as Women of Color must be willing to support, love, and nurture other Women of Color. It is not a choice but rather it is an imperative. We must put an end to all of the self-hate, jealousy, and competition amongst each other. We must move beyond being brainwashed into thinking some of us are "better" because we may be a few shades lighter, have a softer grade of hair, live in a mansion, or God blessed has us with a better education yielding greater wealth.

So what? Many people have everything and feel completely empty inside. Many others are struggling and barely making ends meet and have more gratitude and contentment in their current position. We are all one in the same. We are all we have. No other race will take ownership of this critical responsibility. No other race can understand what it feels like to embrace our skin, walk in our shoes, and experience the trials and triumphs of a Woman of Color. Only what you do for Christ will last. Nothing else in life matters. Here are some examples of what "you" can do to help build up your fellow sisters in Christ:

1. Empower (Give her wisdom on "survival of the fittest" based on obedience to God and consistency with follow through).
2. Emulate (Teach her to be better than you by using your Godly lifestyle as the example).
3. Encourage (Strengthen her when she is weak. Cry with her, laugh with her, and hold her if needed).
4. Enrich (Teach her to stay connected to the word of God to stay Full on Life).
5. Enlighten (Remind her of the endless possibilities available to her if she chooses to walk in her purpose and serve God wholeheartedly).

SonKiss Affirmation:
I will help to build up my sisters in Christ by …

(Fill in the blank with your personal statement. Repeat aloud several times until you believe it and commit to it. Post the message on your wall or mirror.)

Chapter 24

X- Go the eXtra Mile

"Whatever you do, work heartily, as for the Lord and not for men, knowing that from the Lord you will receive the inheritance as your reward. You are serving the Lord Christ."
-Colossians 3:23-24 (ESV)

Reflection Question:
   (1) What must you be willing to do (start, stop, change, or maintain) to Go the eXtra Mile?

Women of Color have been blessed and highly favored by an eXtraordinary God! Thus, we have been given limitless potential to "Go the eXtra Mile." Whenever we learn of all the great parables about our Savior, He always stood out from the crowd as a beacon of light and hope, a miracle worker, a representation of unconditional love, truth, and righteousness, and our greatest example of perseverance (dying on the cross).

Our Lord and Savior Christ was different, daring, bold, and rejected the path of least resistance. He consistently chose to Go the eXtra Mile when He could have said no thank you but I'll pass. He chose to be diligent, consistent, persistent, and faithful in spite of the many obstacles, rejection, ridicule, and suffering He faced during his entire lifetime.

He never stopped. He never gave up or gave in to temptation. He never wavered or faltered. He chose to make difficult sacrifices even when others He trusted failed Him. He chose to make going the eXtra Mile His standard.

Although we are imperfect beings, I challenge all women of color to strive to be like Christ in all your ways. We must be willing to go the eXtra Mile by:

1. Working with integrity and full competency

2. Saying and doing what others will not do. Be willing to get your hands dirty and sacrifice time, money, etc.

3. Stop waiting on others and avoid following the crowd. Choose to create your own path (Do it yourself).

4. Maintaining godly standards when we are behind closed doors and no one is watching.

5. Putting in the eXtra: volunteer, give, serve, share, and love.

SonKissed Praise Report

I am so thankful to my mother (Cookie) for inspiring me to go the eXtra Mile. This chapter is dedicated to her for being my earthly (godly) example for over 20 years. The lessons and blessings she poured into me are the reason I am alive and well today. Her seeds (words and actions) speak to my heart daily and I find myself measuring my life choices against her Godly standards.

From maintaining the upkeep of our home, paying bills (on time), mowing the lawn (had to be done the right way), dressing to impress, serving her family, church, and community, and spending quality time with the Lord (main priority) and her family, my mother embodied the characteristics of being wise, meticulous, strategic, and that "you" are responsible for your success.

My mother taught me to speak up, believe in me, and follow through because no one else will do it for me. My love for writing and inspiring women of color would not exist if not for my mother encouraging me to discover my passion and keep pursuing it until I exceed my expectations. She also laid the foundation that preparation, consistency, and failure are required to reach successful outcomes. You must be willing to fail until you discover what will keep you successful, then keep repeating the process (remembering to be patient, flexible, and open to God changing and growing in you which may alter the process but for the better).

I pray that my words will help to empower other women of color who will carry the torch and empower more each other as my mother empowered me.

SonKiss Affirmation:
I will go the eXtra Mile by…

(Fill in the blank with your personal statement. Repeat aloud several times until
you believe it and commit to it. Post the message on your wall or mirror.)

Chapter 25

Y- Share "Your Story" (Your Words of Empowerment)

"Well-spoken words bring satisfaction; well-done work has its own reward."-Prov. 12:14
"Words satisfy the mind as much as fruit does the stomach; good talk is as gratifying as a good harvest. Words kill, words give life; you choose."- Prov. 18:20-21 (MSG)

Reflection Questions:
(1) What does "Your Story" say about you? Is there anything you would like to change? If so, what will you change? How will you change?
(2) How can sharing "Your Story" help you and other women of color?

As women of color, we have the creative power to use our words to heal or to kill. Your life story has the potential to save, set free, sever ungodly relationships, and allow Women of color the power to soar like an eagle. Every single detail of your life is significant and has purpose attached to it. God has the ability to use every part of you (successes, failures, skills, talents, abilities, experiences, and weaknesses) for the up building of His Kingdom.

Your story is needed to leave an impact on the many lives that are predestined to cross your path. Yes, someone else's destination for greatness is dependent upon you doing your part by sharing your story. Thus, if you fail to follow through, you negatively impact the lives of many generations to come.

Women of color must be willing to be honest and transparent with each other about the social issues and injustices we face and how to deal with them on a regular basis. No sugarcoating, lying, placating, rationalizing, or telling us what you "think" we want to hear, please. God always makes a way out of no way. There is always a positive resolution (ram in the thicket) if we will unify, communicate, and collaborate with each other using our gifts to heal our nation.

We must be willing to speak the truth in love. We must share the entire story (the victories, the losses, the ups and downs, the pretty and ugly parts, the secrets, the mistakes, the close calls, when we got caught, times when we fell short, and when we got back up).

Choose to fully embrace and celebrate your story. I encourage all women of color to think before you speak and choose your words wisely. Choose words that will uplift, inspire, motivate, encourage, love and support, correct, and promote positive change for the better. Always ensure that your words and actions are in alignment with the things of God. And remember to speak words of life to yourself at all times.

SonKiss Affirmation:
I will share my story and empower my
sister by…

(Fill in the blank with your personal statement.
Repeat aloud several times until you believe it
and commit to it. Post the message on your
wall or mirror.)

Chapter 26

Z-Zest and Zeal Seals the Deal

"Don't burn out; keep yourselves fueled and aflame. Be alert servants of the Master, cheerfully expectant. Don't quit in hard times; pray all the harder. Help needy Christians; be inventive in hospitality." - Romans 12: 11-13 (MSG)

Reflection Question:
   (1) How are you choosing to live your life with Zest and Zeal for Christ? What message does your life speak to the world?

According to Merriam Webster's Online Dictionary, the word, zest is defined as a lively excitement or a feeling of enjoyment and enthusiasm. Zeal refers to a feeling of strong eagerness or a positive feeling of wanting to push ahead with something.

Women of color must continually strive for both zest and zeal for Christ abundant living. Although this book is focused on women of color being blessed with success, success is *not* the ultimate reward.

The ultimate reward lies in life fulfillment in Christ. Don't get it twisted. Our life is not about us but all about Christ using our lives as His example. Why were you born? What has God called you to do? Success is more of the icing on the cake and a result of us reaping from what we have sown in our lives. Thus, we are called to not only finish strong but to finish what

God started in us (no matter how many times we fail or how long it takes to reach our destiny). We are not promised a job tomorrow. We are not promised our health tomorrow. We are not promised tomorrow. We must enjoy and savor every moment of this journey today and every day.

We must choose to live life to the full every day with zest and zeal for the Lord! Living with zest and zeal involves us finding fresh and new ways to keep our life journey full of fervor, spontaneity, and excitement by choosing adventures, challenges, and new hobbies.

This allows God to using our life as a message of joy, hope, and inspiration to others. Our living should reflect the light of Christ. Many of our relationships fail miserably because we become boring, complacent, and extremely predictable. We must keep others smiling, laughing, and sometimes even guessing or on their toes.

Choose to live fully by taking risks, seizing opportunities disguised as problems or unmet needs, stepping outside of our comfort zone by doing something you've never done or thought you could do, being the change agent you are hoping for, and opening your eyes, ears, hearts, and minds to things, places, and people who are different from you. We must be eager and willing to arise and live each day with passion and purpose to make a difference in the lives of others.

Women of color, please keep believing, praying, tithing, repenting of your sins, speaking the word, sharing and teaching the gospel, praising His name, going to church, participating in ministry and fellowship with other believers, and spending quality time with Christ. Do these things with continual zest and zeal and Christ will "seal the deal" by rewarding you with uncommon favor, success, and blessings beyond measure for being obedient to His will and purpose for your life.

SonKiss Affirmation:
I will maintain my zest and zeal for the Lord by…
(Fill in the blank with your personal statement. Repeat aloud several times until you believe it and commit to it. Post the message on your wall or mirror.)

Acknowledgements

First and foremost, I want to thank my Lord and Savior, Jesus Christ for blessing me beyond measure.

I would like to thank my father, Horace Mitchell, for loving and supporting me all the days of my life.

I want to thank all of my family members, especially my brothers, sister, and host of nieces and nephews who have all inspired me to reach my best.

I want to thank all of my friends, church members, and fellow entrepreneurs who have encouraged me with words of wisdom and motivation to never quit. Special thanks to my best friends LaDonna Evans and Brenett Dickerson who helped to keep me humble, hungry, and accountable.

I want to also thank my mentors: Dr. Nina Bronner, Dr. Venus Reese, Oprah Winfrey, Michelle Obama, Valorie Burton, and the list goes on and on.

For anyone I forgot to mention (too many of you to name), you know who you are and I greatly appreciate your support.

About the Author

Tracy Mitchell is an empowerment life speaker with a background in nursing; training and development; coaching and mentoring; and creative writing. She is also the founder of "*TeeMitchellSpeaks*", a personal blog and website dedicated to empowering women to create and discover the "hidden" value in everything they possess (skills, talents, abilities, experiences, and weaknesses).

Tracy Mitchell believes in speaking about life, biblical principles, health and wellness, and purpose to help women live invincible and intentional leading to total life fulfillment. She is equipped with the skillsets required to enrich women physically, mentally, spiritually, and emotionally resulting in healing and wholeness.

You can stay in touch with Ms. Mitchell by emailing her at **www.teemitchellspeaks.com**.

Notes